Echoes

A collection of poems

Anvi Tongia

Made with ❤ on the Notion Press Platform

www.notionpress.com

For Shreshtha,

it is in your arms I find infinity.

Table Of Contents

In Loving Memory 1
The Blank Page Screams a Million Words 3
Urban Train of Thoughts..5
Before I'm Gone..7
On the Kitchen Floor..9
The Whistling 11
I Dig up a Grave for No One 13
Love? 15
For a Moment..17
Rose in the Glass-room..19
The Curious Case of Cinderella 21
Echoes..23
Time Tragedy..27
Toothache 29
Spellbound 31
Lilac Lullabies..33
Ramp Walk towards Eternity..35
The Robin..37
Rainy Day 39
Who are you? 41
Black and White 43

Birthday Girl 45
Celestial Hell 47
Conversations with the Dark 51
Sixty Days 53
The Lilac Flower 55
Today I'm Choosing to be Happy 57
Teenager in Love 59
Space and Sky 61
The Real Masculinity 63
Firefly 65
She goes by 67
The Dove 69
18th Century Love 71
Backpack Girl 73
A Letter to Forever 75
Under the Streetlight 77
October 79
A Thing Called Night 81
Ms. Baker 83
Rise of a Kingdom 87
Damned Legacy 89
The Moon's a Liar too 91
Twin Flame 93

For Mom 95
The Night is Young 97
Home 101
Butterfly 103
I'm not a Genius.......................................105

Author's Note

Poetry is the song I could listen to forever. I remember waking up on a Sunday morning, and the storm had gathered around the clouds. Nevertheless, I opened my little blue journal and penned down all that I knew and loved. This was among the many instances that, time and time again, remind me why I love the art of poetry the way I do.

This entire process of carefully handpicking poems I've written throughout my little life has been a medley of emotions. The truth stands that this journey from endless tears to finding comfort and confidence in my words has been an insight into growing up.

I believe every hurdle on the way to your ultimate destination is a learning lesson crafted by the universe. Perhaps, not understanding my own emotions was my hurdle between finally letting go of these poems from my little blue journal and putting them out into the world.

My biggest takeaway from this experience of publishing has been being able to come to terms with my vulnerability. These several months in the making of this book have been moments between perplexity, wisdom, pride, and pure bliss.

I've put in my best efforts to lay out these poems in such a manner that hopefully you find a part of yourself among my words.

So sit back, light a candle, and take a look inside your mind. For each word someone writes, it brings you deeper into the stories they hide.

1.

In Loving Memory

In loving memory
Of the innocence she lost
When they took away her words,
Ruptured her quill,
Shattered the bottle of liquid dreams, and
The ink, which stained the very face, she once adorned.

2.

The Blank Page Screams a Million Words

The blank page screams a million words.
The eyes tell a story untold.
The moon shines and teases the stars;
The stars too chase the dark,
not knowing they're the light.
The light flickers till it's nonexistent.
The dark corners the room,
But glows a light from the moon—
Giving its warmth to the heart,
Peace to the mind, and
A voice to the spirit.

Echoes

3.

Urban Train of Thoughts

My train of thoughts
Runs wild, then stops
At a station near daydreams,
In the heart of cement cities.

The skylines get up at four
And the coffee machines begin to roar.
Not one moment to pause
and look up at the stars.

The traffic begins to sweep
The footsteps off the streets.
No sparrows chirp around,
Neither do leaves fall on the ground.

The summer of forever
Doesn't seem as sweet.
Blue yet empty, the river
Still feels incomplete.

4.

Before I'm Gone

I see you dancing in the crowd,
Screaming lyrics to your favourite song.

I take one last glance
Before I'm gone.

I'll ship letters in a bottle to you
On that far-off island
Where flowers bloom,
Where birds sing,
and everything smells like you.

The skyline stands tall—
Blue-gray sky above it all.
The water ripples down below
Unlike anything you've seen before.

You were a dream; I should've known all along.
The people have the same music taste as you.
Why don’t you sing them your favourite song?

I take one last glance
Before I'm gone.

5.

On the Kitchen Floor

I sit wide awake;
A cup of instant anxiety in hand.
How much more could I take,
of the voices arguing in dreamland?

The sea starts to hit the ceiling,
raging its way onto the shore,
wiping out the snug feeling,
and few settlements for evermore.

The moon takes charge;
The outpost is still in hot water.
Restoration is a price overlarge;
It was time to close the border.

The thought pauses there
And strives to unbolt another door,
But my mind takes me nowhere
as I sit on the kitchen floor.

6.

The Whistling

The whistling continues
Haunting the night.
The air filled with blues,
Minds with fright.

Dreams left distort,
Visions blurred,
Eyes filled with salt—
Silence, not a word.

7.

I Dig up a Grave for No One

I dig up a grave
For no one.
None to lie
So, it lies open.
It gives a sense of security:
A place of our own,
Nothing but land
And grass overgrown.
A pretty stone stands tall;
My name engraved
And "A loving person,"
It says.
The flowers remain
A few days.
They too rot
And turn grey.

My bones still lie
And look up at the sky,
Not from curious eyes
But communicate through goodbyes.

8.

Love?

Maybe it's an open door,
Maybe a watertight ballroom
With the chandelier hung high
on the verge of breaking down.

Maybe their souls intertwine,
And every touch replenishes the emotions long lost.
The room floods with nerves and every spirit is there to cheer you on,
But a little unsurety lingers on your lips,
Looking for the right words every time you converse with him.
Your curious eyes look for love in his.

The little things stay with you,
Forever embedded in your brain.
A little hope for meaning and being
understood,
To see and to be seen,
To cry and laugh and fight through,
To break down the water-tight walls and soar,
And to be reborn with passion
every time your eyes find his looking back at
you.

9.

For a Moment

For a moment I believed it;
I let myself live.
Far from fear and walls of morals,
For a moment, I let go and breathed through.
Not short breaths of terror but breathing out of fulfillment.
Between the cold breeze and nights full of darkness,
The one glowing giant stood out,
Following me wherever I went.
He did not change with time or with a different social group.
He was there through it all—
The tears, the smiles, the chaos, and the silence.
For a moment the voices stopped.
It was just the wind and I
In our own little microcosmos.

10.

Rose in the Glass-room

Its mystic musings unfold;
Petal by petal, it blooms.
Bright and vivid,
In the room of smoke,
It spreads its leaves of autumn hue,
And diffuses its scent of ethereal blasphemy
in the nooks of the six-cornered glass-room.

Never have I ever
Been charmed as such
Of a being of nature.
But, its edges shatter my brittle heart
And leave the pieces to be immortalised,
Bearing witness to divine power.

So, the scent rises
Warming the walls,
But they shiver of fragile foundations
And still holding onto misty dreams,
The walls stand.

11.

The Curious Case of Cinderella

She crashed her glass slipper on that bedroom wall
Then burned the hall down.
Her fury raged into flames of the fire
That lit the castle walls.
She erased her perfect fairytale—
Even the poisoned apple went stale.
And, knocking down the doors of her civility,
She began her journey towards necessary hostility.

12.

Echoes

Delicacies of lands unknown
Spread on the grey linen
And each sip of Merlot
Muddled the chamber.

A toast is raised
By the gentleman in black,
"to the glorious 20s,"
And then the goblet cracks.

Laying shattered on the tiled floor,
The shards reflect a lantern,
Which paid witness
to youth, this room once wore.

The hourglass ran short of stardust
And turned the spilled unconsciousness
To elixir of love.

The shoes fiddled and fussed
Finding heads to crown culpable.
And, among the hollow chaos
Of gluttonous men and snobbish fellows,
All that remained
Were echoes.

13.

The Flame

A flame battling for its last breath
Diffuses its melancholic scent
Over the grave silence.

It glows and burns
With all its might
And serves justice
With its livid light.

And, pearls of fragrance
Take their daint form
Around borders
Of the wax-like storm.

And, with ashes of woe,
It takes its final bow
And remains timeless, forevermore.

14.

Time Tragedy

Shouldn't it be simple like the past?
Not torture like today.
Would it be different, my future?
Or all just the same?

Memories came,
The past forgave
My mistakes, not my case.
Could it be happier,
My later days?
My past forgotten;
My mind kept sane.

15.

Toothache

The after-pain lingers in the cavity;
Blood forced shut with cotton.
Two gone two more to go—
Teeth that shall never be restored.
A needle of some fluid
Supposed to prevent blood rain:
Just an illusion—
the needle, not the pain.
Picked out bones from my smile,
Bones that shall now lie rotten and remain forgotten.

Echoes

16.

Spellbound

I brewed this love in a cauldron
And sung across woods
Bewitching his mind.

He brings me sunflowers.

I could dwell around roses.

Daisies are what bring me joy.

Bouquets, what a perfect ploy.

I paint the moon
in rainbow colours,
Create his perfect palette,
And leave him solid.

My mask drops.

I reach out my hand.

He takes off his armour.

He's quite the charmer.

He wears darker colours now—
a crow on a chromatic low.

I wear him like a crown;
I've got him spellbound.

17.

Lilac Lullabies

In your hymns of sleep,
The world stopped spinning.

The hymn grows louder
With the fall of each cloud
And my eyelids start to drop.

The stars shut down
One by one;
Your eyes lit up the whole room.

I pull on my covers
And watch you depart.

Your crown breaks in swift, slow movements,
Landing on the floor of velvet dreams.

You little hoax of comfort
Was perhaps, just insanity.

But, the lullabies of lilac hover
And put me into deep slumber.
Far from your agony,
I dream in periwinkle hues.
The lens fogs up with a lavender blush,
But the truth lies—
No price is colossal enough
To bring back the fire you alight.

Among crimsons and golds,
Among teals and indigos,
In between worlds of mulberry and wine—
Only, does lilac bring to end
My stormy night.

18.

Ramp Walk towards Eternity

The edge taunts you to take a leap;
It tests your patience
And makes you yearn for comfort.

Your greatest secrets linger in the forefront of your mind,

Waiting to be screamed out in the distance
To rid yourself of the weight of power,
To leave you vulnerable with your shame,
Your regret, and your innocence.

So the heart rebels and makes the feet unstable.
With joy, you dive.

The wind breaks your shams
And leaves you broken to be rebuilt,

To be made rock solid,

To be reborn breakable and with the phoenix's perpetuity.

You armour up for battle,

Knowing nothing and everything about your opponent— you.

In a grain of the hourglass,

You make your destiny.

The edge taunts you to take a leap,

pulls you out of your snug sleep,

And sets in stone your ramp walk towards

eternity.

19.

The Robin

The little bird with angel wings
Had never once tried
To be more than its mere self.
But today that fear of holding back, died.

The robin soars across the blue expanse
With salt filling its lungs,
Holding on to a red thread of hope,
and the might to become someone.

It marches right into the sky
With a heart beating out its chest
And felt more than it ever did,
Becoming more than its mere self.

Echoes

20.

Rainy Day

Looking out the window,
With rain slowly drizzling down,
My emotions overflow.
I've never been one to cry out loud
Or profess how I've been feeling.
I never liked the rain,
Yet I feel myself healing.

The low rumbles in the sky,
Bright lightning strikes,
And the pitter-patter of rain,
to me, still remain mundane.

Don't worry though!
It's all in my head.

Maybe I'm a little colour blind
and a little out of my mind—
Don't see the magic people see
When from the clouds, rain flees.
But I made the sky my canvas,
My words the paint.
With brush strokes of passion,
I paint away!

21.

Who are you?

"Who are you?"
Asked the girl in the mirror.
I'm you, I replied.
"Why aren't you thinner?"
She looked surprised.
"Why do you look the way you do?"

I wish I could tell her
That I won't be taller
That I can't sing or dance
Or just take a chance.
Maybe she understands me;
Perhaps, she does not.
Who will ever know?

I look back at the girl and
This time she looked perfect.

She asked me once again,
“Who are you?”

“I’m not you,” I said.
“I have my flaws
And I recognise them.”

22.

Black and White

Black are articles with sorrow—
The nightfall, the grave, the crow.

White takes a different stand—
The moon, the wedding dress, the land of sand.

Although sharp as a sword,
I wouldn't take white word for word.

The misunderstood pinnacle of life—
Its name is "Black," I'm told.

A diamond shines in shades of both—
Born from black and molded into white.
A true advocate of nature's growth.

In life then, which shall we choose
From the rainbow stack?
White's tranquil view
Or the vindictive black?

Perhaps, the dilemma shall never cease.
In lieu, we must increase
our tolerance towards one
And humility to the other.
Maybe fuse the polars
and live in grey composure.

23.

Birthday Girl

The clock struck twelve and the day had begun.
A little girl was now a woman.
That night she was Sleepless;
Society's rules seemed needless.
Cake and pudding graced the meal;
Bliss was all she could feel.

She learned to be Fearless but still a Queen—
Sincere, polite, kind, and keen,
Was bold and brave, knew how to fight,
Could raze darkness and find light.

I am enough she pondered.
It was self-love that made her stronger.
And just like that the day was over,
it would repeat next year and that was closure.

24.

Celestial Hell

I screamed as if you'd come back.
You didn't even turn around.
Your shadow changed as the sun tilted.
Your silhouette departed the view
And then circled back like the moon.

Vivid and tormenting to the eye,
Every time
You look over with
More and more lies.

Is there another North star
In your solar systemic mind?
Or did I become Pluto,
Amongst the night sky?

You were the sky with stars,
With light and the dark.
My favourite celestial muse;
The cure to all my blues.

Then you turned and never returned.
Your eyes red with tears,
Flowed like meteors in the void—
Meteors, which left us destroyed.

It gut me at first and then slowly I grew
Out of your arms and sight,
Out of your mind,
And remained at peace with my rotten life.

I'll remain forever the spirit of a Robin,
Believing you saw reason beyond compare.
Did you see the despair in my iris,
The ones reflecting your name?

Regrets, loss, desire, disdain—
All mixed in a dreamy cauldron of vains.
I toast to the final solemn dwell
And make my escape from your celestial hell.

Echoes

25.

Conversations with the Dark

Conversations with the dark
On a vulnerability pill,
Shut out the stars
And the November chill.

The inner child screams
And the sky tears open;
All the little mind deals
Lay eternally broken.

In solemn peace,
The tears flow;
The moonlight burns,
but the stars bring hope.

26.

Sixty Days

Sixty days and counting
Of the silence I set in our story.
The mind pierces my heart
With each replaying image
Defaming your glory.
Sixty days, before I engraved,
In the pages of history,
This cruel flame.

As midnight falls,
my heart pens down
the last words of a weeping soul.
Not once since then,
Did my grieving quill take your name.

27.

The Lilac Flower

The lilac flower lies
And blooms in daylight.
It looks up at the lush skies
And hopes with all its might.
It teases the rays of gold
Until it gets cloned.

Forever it will wait,
Hiding from the rain,
But Instead drenched in gay,
Slowly it will decay
And become nothing again.

28.

Today I'm Choosing to be Happy

Today I'm choosing to be happy
Because tomorrow may not be well.
There's no reason to stay unhappy, when
Snails come out of their shells.
Darkness will decline by a single ray of light,
Birds will make their flight
Across seas
To spread peace.
Trees will blossom
And remain evergreen.

29.

Teenager in Love

The waves hit the beach;
Summer fever was high.
I grinned through my eyes—
You and I felt like paradise.

Summer lulls by your smiles,
Daylight warms the dull skies,
Moons change every night,
But my heart, it stays in paradise.

“I won’t be staying forever,”
She’d say.
“Oh, we’ll freeze May then,
And put it on replay.”

Rather, I'd have you break my heart
And say this would never last.
It'll give me a sense of relief—
All this wasted chemistry.

So pack up your bags
And leave me longing.
Never look back
Because I won't be crying.

Summer lulled by your smiles,
The sun warmed the dull skies,
Moons changed every night,
But my heart stayed in paradise.

Eternity with you would've been divine;
Grateful I am that our paths intertwined.
Indeed, "forever" favours the tough,
But I'm just a teenager in love.

30.

Space and Sky

A celestial gathering takes place tonight;
I shall witness it upon twilight.
The many orbs of fire, belts of ice,
A pole star shines ever so bright.

I wish to see the meteors racing through the sky.
I wish to feel the moon's pseudo-light on my skin,
White, it shines in the air as if it flies.

Oh, What fun it is to see shimmering giants
When they fly across oceans and seas,
As if they have somewhere to be.

31.

The Real Masculinity

Hear him
Before you define his masculinity.
His strength is more than just muscle.
His heart beats out of love.
He smiles in good faith
And cries when it hurts.
His worth is more than just your
Supposed manliness
And his spirit is not bound by your ideals of manhood.

So, before you tell him what a man is,
Know that a man is what he makes of himself—
Sensitive yet strong,
Has a sense of right and wrong,
Is kind and placid to his core.
The one you stereotype him to be—
A man is so much more.

32.

Firefly

Under the somber sunlight,
With its wings of delicacy,
The firefly took flight
towards eternal ecstasy.

In every fashion arcane,
Still longing for simplicity,
The firefly knew all but urbane
And its ensuing destiny.

The flashing city lights
Outshine her little heart
And accepting defeat,
She returns to play her part.

There glows a force,
Mighty like the sea,
From the corners of abandonment
and buoyant glee.

But the creatures of words,
As her line deceases,
Trap her dainty spirit
For their centerpieces.

33.

She goes by

Death, she intrigues me.
Not a lot of her I see.
She comes once in a while,
Around me.
Like a grey, misty shadow hovering in the sky;
Takes all, in the blink of an eye.
I want to see her, but not.
Once I do, I'll get caught.
She'll take lives and be on her way–
Town to town, bay to bay.
She'll come as a disease
Or an unfortunate event.
She won't think and then cease;
Lives could have been well spent.
She's quite just in some way.
Her victim could be anyone, any day.
To her, everyone's the same.

The dead lie,
Feel no pain.
She's still in the sky.
Do you know her name?
"Death," she goes by.

34.

The Dove

The dove in white
Soars through the blue skies.

Peace she preaches
Because the war when it comes,
Will leave men undone.

Their spirits burned to the ground
With nothing for, to stick around.

Then will the dove sit around and watch,
The world fall apart.

For egos, conflicts, and facades
Have left the system flawed.

To make a state without war
Where peace is loved more,
Still holding her beacon of hope,
She rises each dawn.

35.

18th Century Love

The smiles came to a conclusion;
The strings played along with the banter;
Prancing about the 18th-century ballroom,
Marked the beginning of their new chapter.

The little maiden twirled with joy
As the hymn of the string quartet reverberated.
The Prince caught a glint of euphoria in her eyes
And knew this serendipity was fated.

He forces his feet on the dance floor
And with his heart of nerves
Offers his hand,
Not knowing it was already hers.

She leads;
Along, he glides.
Euphoria—
Filled his own eyes.

The chandelier revolved,
The clock hands turned,
And in those eyes of hopeless love,
She saw his heart burn.

36.

Backpack Girl

In the shade of a grey-haired tree,
Sits a carefree soul
With her eyes squinting in joy
And heart smiling of love.

A spring-blossom blouse
Compliments the blush on her cheeks
And her face lights up
In line with the lanterns,
hanging from the arms of the tree.

This forsaken poet wonders
What musings cross her mind:
Bothers of the world
Or how her stars aligned.

She embodies the elegance
Of a freshwater pearl.
Oh, how my heart remains entangled
with the backpack girl.

37.

A Letter to Forever

Forever,
you're a long time.
Am I to call you mine?
That essence smelling divine
Of peppermint and lime.

You fall fresh as dawn
And cast sage and calm.

At dusk, you’re quite fine,
Impelling the stars to align.
Bells of midnight further chime
And the land reeks of roses and wine.

For in your little hoax,
The folk call it a blissful time.

38.

Under the Streetlight

Two figures stand in the shadows,
Blurred by the ochre street light.
A rare sight of love,
Which didn't fade with daylight.

A maiden laughs;
The other caresses her cheek.
Identical Chelsea boots
Cover their cold feet.

The brunette walks crooked—
Drunk on the night.
The other, redhead,
Holds her upright.

They walk and walk
For years to come
And their peppermint perfume
Washes over the city's gloom.

The pavement remembers their footsteps
And indents them with rain.
They returned one day,
Having taken each other's name.

39.

October

October, your spirit glides;
The winds let go and
Your heart smiles.

The lush grounds perish,
In the way of men who dwell
And the town goes desolate
With rings of the midnight bell.

Now rotten and overlooked,
The coffee-tinted leaves lie
And with each passing day,
Endure the dry spell that runs them by.

Of all beings of fall,
One catches my eye.
She's alluring in her ways-
An angel who descends from the sky.

40.

A Thing Called Night

In its entirety, the night is a maverick.
It dawns in its time and lets go of all civility,
Pulls a cover over its timid other half,
And lets the light guide the way to its heart.

Damned it will be,
When it brings to surface
All its humility.

41.

Ms. Baker

She has a funny accent
And a limp in her walk;
She's of British descent
Or perhaps she's a scot.

She drives an old minivan
In the ugliest colour of gray.
Last summer she had a tan,
About which there's nothing more to say.

She owns a tabby cat,
who, last winter ran away.
As a replacement, she adopted a bat,
Who came out in the day.

She bakes cookies every Tuesday
And adds salt instead of sugar;
The taste, although it fades,
Funny is the mixed liquor.

She runs along the street
With a half-torn hat.
You always see her bare feet
And that is all about that.

What can I say about Ms. Baker?
She's an erratic lady.
Unfortunately, she's my neighbour
So, I've gotten used to her already.

On Sundays, she watches her favourite
telenovela
And discusses town gossip with the birds.
She’s a real Cinderella,
Until it comes to doing the actual work.

She had a daughter ages ago,
Who ran away with an elderly man
And once in a while sends a postcard from Cairo
Saying, “Hello!” from her and Stan.

Ms. Baker makes a lovely date
Until of course, you show up late.
I remember her kicking out ‘What's his name?’
All Because he refused to shave.

Oh, beautiful Ms. Baker,
If only they accepted middle-aged imbeciles in beauty pageants,
You'd be quite the groundbreaker;
After all, No one can match your talents.

What more can I say about Ms. Baker?
She's funky with her tunes.
She’d be selling out stadiums,
If pop culture worshipped buffoons.

Don't get me wrong,
Her heart is made up of gold.
She's fun to have along,
As long as you do exactly what you're told.

I suggest you acquaint yourself with her ways,
Her different shades of violet, pink, and blue.
My fondness for her grows every day
And I'm sure you'll love her too.

42.

Rise of a Kingdom

Born out of chaos,
the kingdom marks itself on the map
With its closest allies
Standing shouldered to her.

She dreams of power,
Schemes rebellion,
And breeds imperial glory
From the corners of her hell,
Raises demons in her basement,
Who stand guard on trapdoors,
Screening the nobodies and
Declaring worthy the somebodies.

She cries in the grand halls
With the lady of the town.

With knives piercing her back,
She bleeds in tears of loss,
Sings a song of faith
And invokes the spirits
that fortify her mighty throne.

Like the ocean's rise, she upsurges,
Composes her Battlecry
With the golden feather of destiny,
And lets the nectar flow towards infinity.

43.

Damned Legacy

I dream a little dream
Of breaking glass windows
With hairbrushes.

I dream of carrying a shovel in hand,
Screaming as if I'd burst into flames.

It's a fancy game.

My closet is a graveyard
Of all my past selves.

It refurbishes time and time again.

In my black robe,
I run wild
In my mind.

Hellfire rains at dawn
In its typical way.
I stand stripped of civility
And win the devil's child play.

Confinement seems too glorious;
I'd rather have thorns in my eyes.
I'll cry rivers of regret,
Which fill up my cup of wine.

I keep a glass quill,
In my back pocket,
To write footnotes in my destiny
On the very stone walls
Of my damned legacy.

44.

The Moon's a Liar too

The light fails to breakthrough
And quietly hovers like the moon.
It fails to shine and
steals another's spotlight.
After all, the moon's a liar too.

Painted in mourning,
The clouds belt a dirge
And upon the pink morning,
The light begins to resurge.

I light a match
And attract thousands of other flames.
They spark up my eyes
And clear the colourless skies.

I look up with a knowingness.

Tell the moons and stars
To stay dark tonight.
I'm going to be my own light.

45.

Twin Flame

Clouds envelop the moon;
The birds carry a sacred tune.
Two girls dance in the wind,
Forsaking everything.

The night throws a feast;
The dark remains deceased.
The light within glints
And their hearts begin to sprint.

Worries shed away,
As under the stars they lay.
They converse not of the future
but live in today.

The moon tells a tale
And their dream ships sail.
A promise for forever—
To live life whenever.

Breezes fly by.
A thick fog covers the sky.
Mystery, this moment shall be—
Recorded all in memory.

Guilty pleasures please,
Even the stars agree—
However small the night may be,
May the effect last forever and remain pain-
free.

46.

For Mom

She laughs and the world stops.
She cries and my heart cries with her.
She stands with confidence
And my mind is able to conquer all.

Mom,

Your doe eyes stitch every wound
My mind tears open.

Your faith has mine interwoven.

If you read this, do not cry.
My strength comes from your smile.

47.

The Night is Young

Swish, flowed the air
Carrying within its fold
A message of care—
"Keep going on," it spoke.

Among city lights,
The moon hangs
Shining like the knight
In my royal dreamland.

The night sky flutters,
Warning its departure.
The stars then mutter,
"Until tomorrow, sweetheart."

But the night is young,
And so is my mind.
So, I go on revelling
My wasted time.

“I'll grow up tomorrow,”
I promise myself.
There's still the world to experience,
Why limit oneself?

I make friends with the wind
And fall in love with its liberty.
I chase the night
And its never ending mystery.

I'm a creature of the clock,
But for once, I let go.
I sit on the side of the street
And admire the moon's glow.

I hop on a bus to nowhere
And let the wine whisk me away.
When my senses will return,
Who's to say.

Every stop
brings a new escape.
Next morning,
I only remember the magic of the cityscape.

48.

Home

Dance like tomorrow's fiction.
Make the clock take a break
To watch the smiles spread.
A million miles to go
Before the great climb.
So, get lost
for a night.

Open your heart a little
And let the love sink in;
It feels like home—
All their grins.
Before you set out into the world,
Shining your own light,
Absorb the warmth from others'
And stay home
Just for one night.

49.

Butterfly

Born out of confinement, she soars,
Spreads her wings with hope
And in search of belonging travels to the ends of the sky—
Always dreaming, always reaching for more.

She is the girl in the coffee shop,
The one in the bookstore,
And the one who used to lock up her bedroom door.

She's grown up now,
Used to the screams
And numb to the rattles.
No metaphor deep enough
To explain it,
But she finally learned
To win her own battles.

50.

I'm not a Genius

I'm not a genius.
I'm just a dreamer.

I wake up with fuddled feelings
And suffocating brain ceilings.

I lie awake through the stormy night
With nothing but candlelight.

I write on ruled pages
Within my diary's navy blue cages.

I try my best to make people laugh.
I try to always capture the perfect photograph.

I go quiet in loud spaces
And I run wild in imaginary races.

I have so much more to say, always.
And my heart melts, when I'm praised.

What more do I say?
I try to grow my mind every day.

I try and try and try;
I've made peace with my mind
And the way it cries.

I run out of rhymes
All the time.

I write words on a page
Because I can't say them to your face.

I'm glass half-empty one day
And the next, I'm a believer.

I'm not a genius.
I'm just a dreamer.

Echoes

www.ingramcontent.com/pod-product-compliance
Lightning Source LLC
LaVergne TN
LVHW041113150826
845673LV00007B/2033

* 9 7 9 8 8 9 1 3 3 4 7 7 9 *